THE BEARS' ALMANAC

A Year in Bear Country...

holidays

seasons

weather

actual facts about snow, wind, rain, thunder, lightning, the sun, the moon... and lots more

by Stan and Jan Berenstain

Beginner Books • A Division of Random House

Copyright © 1973 by Stanley and Janice Berenstain. All rights reserved under International and Pan-American Copyright Conventions. Published in the United States by Random House, Inc., New York, and simultaneously in Canada by Random House of Canada Limited, Toronto. Manufactured in the United States of America.
Library of Congress Cataloging in Publication Data: Berenstain, Stanley. The bears' almanac. SUMMARY: The further adventures of the Bear family also include information on holidays, weather, and the seasons. [1. Bears—Stories. 2. Seasons—Fiction. 3. Stories in rhyme] I. Berenstain, Janice, joint author.   II. Title.
PZ7.B4483Baf   [Fic]   73-2298   ISBN 0-394-82693-0   ISBN 0-394-92693-5 (lib. bdg.)

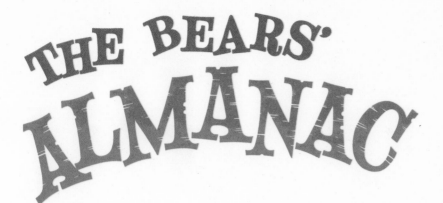

THE BEARS' ALMANAC

A Year in Bear Country

What makes a year?

Four Seasons. Four is all.
Winter, Spring, Summer, Fall.

Twelve Months. A lot to say.
January, February,
March, April, May.
June, July,
August, September.
October, November
and December.

ACTUAL FACTUAL BEAR

How will you know
which season is here?
Come and we'll show you
a Bear Country year.

A brand new calendar!
Hooray! Hooray!
A whole new year
starts today!

In the very first month
on the very first day . . .

is what we say.

The first three months of the year are **WINTER**

JANUARY   FEBRUARY   MARCH

HOW WILL YOU KNOW IT'S WINTER?

Your knees shiver.

You see ice on the river.

Your breath shows.

You've got a
runny nose.

You have to wear a scarf and cap.

Great Natural Bear
starts his
LONG winter nap.

Good night, Small Bear.

See you next Spring.

GREAT
NATURAL
BEAR'S
LAIR

Papa puts on long underwear.

There are
fat snowflakes in the air.

13

The red in the thermometer starts to fall. Sometimes there's hardly any red at all.

Brrr!
IT'S WINTER!

ACTUAL FACTS ABOUT
SNOW

When it's cold
the clouds freeze.
Clouds turn into flakes of ice.
The ice flakes fall . . .
That's **snow.**
Children think it's nice.

ACTUAL FACTUAL BEAR

Some places have no snow,
you'll find.
Children there
don't seem to mind.

In sunny places
such as these,
it's just too hot
for clouds to freeze.

Sometimes snow
comes and goes in a hurry.

When snow does that . . .

it's called a **flurry**.

A **blizzard** . . .

That is what we call
a really, really
BIG snowfall.

You may see it flurry.
You may see it fly . . .
But there's more to snow
than meets the eye.

ACTUAL
FACTUAL
BEAR

You are different
from your sisters and brothers.

And EVERY snowflake
is different from the others.

That is a very nice
thing to know
the next time you are
watching snow.

15

sick in bed

nose drops

brand new sled

belly flops

spinning wheels

snowmobiles

He can skate
a figure eight.

Say! Look what
she can do . . .
six thousand
nine hundred
thirty-two!

18

DEAD MAN'S HILL

What a spill!

ski run

ski lift

snowshoes   snowdrift

This snow is very, very deep.

Great Natural Bear is still asleep!

ZZZZZ

GREAT NATURAL BEAR'S LAIR

FEBRUARY 14

VALENTINE'S DAY

In February,
on Valentine's Day...

I LOVE YOU IS WHAT WE SAY

I Love You

But . . . if you're shy . . .
GUESS WHO
will do.

The next three months of the year are SPRING

APRIL · MAY · JUNE

HOW WILL YOU KNOW IT'S SPRING?

There is slush and mush from melting snow.

Birds sing.
Plants grow.

A crocus grows
right through
the snow.

Wind blows hats off people's heads.

We take out bikes.
We put back sleds.

It's time to get out
brooms and mops.

It starts to rain . . .

then it stops.

The sun begins
to warm the air.

Nice
day,
Small Bear.

Great Natural Bear
comes out
of his lair . . .

GREAT
NATURAL
BEAR'S
LAIR

Hooray!
IT'S SPRING!

25

The first day in April
is APRIL FOOL'S DAY.

Your friends will try
to fool you today.
Here are some of the
things they will say . . .

There's a bug
on your nose!

Your shoes
are not tied!

There's a hole
in your pants!

There's a big purple
monster outside!!

Of course there isn't
a bug
on your nose.

There's no hole
in your pants.

And your shoes
are both tied.

And as for big purple monsters . . .

Help! A big purple monster <u>is</u> waiting outside!

27

28

FLYING A KITE . . .

Is a very fine thing
that you and I
can do in Spring .

I'm ready, Dad.
Let me try it.
I'll take it out right now
and fly it!

Not yet, my boy.
Hold on, Son.
First I'll show you
how it's done.

Now, check the string.
You need a lot.
You also need
a windy spot.

But, Papa!
For a kite to sail . . .
doesn't it have
to have a tail?

Yes, Small Bear.
You are learning how.
This nice long tail
goes on right now!

Next, you must know
which way to run.
Watch the wind blow
and go that way, Son.

But, Dad!
Is that way right?
Shouldn't you run
the other way
with a kite?

Right! Here we go!
Hold the kite high!
I'll let out some string
and we'll let 'er fly!

I get it, Dad! . . .
Except for one thing.
Didn't you let out
too much string?

Son, I showed you
how to do it right.
Now why don't you just
go fly your kite?

What you will need.

A good strong kite.
Plenty of string.
A nice long tail.
A day in Spring.

ACTUAL FACTS ABOUT WIND

Air. Air.
It's everywhere.
When it moves

from here ...

to there ...
that's **wind.**

The wind sails boats ...

and paper planes.

It turns windmills ...

and weather vanes.

A weather vane always shows
just which way the wind blows.

A soft, soft wind
blows the trees . . . .
A soft, soft wind
is called a **breeze**.

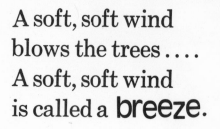

But . . .
Sometimes the wind
is so strong that
it blows off
Farmer Ben Bear's hat.

It blows away
his stool and pail . . . .
THAT kind of wind
is called a **gale**.

A tornado.

A tornado!

That's when
the big wind lifts
poor Farmer Ben.
It lifts him, cow and all,
and then...
It whirls him round
and round again.

It's kind of hard
on Farmer Ben.

There are drops of water
in the clouds.
They are very, very small.
When they get together,
they get big enough
to fall.
That's **rain.**

When just a few
drops fall,
a **drizzle** is what you get.
A drizzle isn't much . . . .
You don't get very wet.

When more
drops fall,
a **shower**
is what you get.
A shower makes you
very wet.

When millions of drops
pour down
a **downpour** is what you get.
A downpour
makes you
SOAKING
wet.

After the rain,
sometimes
a **rainbow** is what you get.

A rainbow is worth
all that wet.

The next three months of the year are

SUMMER

JULY

AUGUST

SEPTEMBER

HOW WILL YOU KNOW IT'S SUMMER?

There's no more school.

CLOSED FOR SUMMER

Papa's in the swimming pool.

40

Mama's making
lemonade.

Granny's sitting
in the shade.

Mosquitoes bite.

You go to bed when
it's still light.

Everybody's very lazy...

except for plants.

They grow like crazy.

The red in the thermometer shoots up tall. There's hardly any room at all.

Phew!
IT'S SUMMER!

ACTUAL FACTS ABOUT THE SUN

ACTUAL FACTUAL BEAR

The sun
is millions
of miles away.
But it works for us
every day.

Farmer Ben's plants
need light and heat
to grow into things
we like to eat.

Sun makes wheat
and corn grow tall.

Without it,
they would not grow
at all.

There would be

no peas...

or beans...

...or tomatoes.

We wouldn't even
have potatoes.

The sun helps potatoes
grow fat and round...
even though
they're
underground.

The sun can turn
a seed this small
into a sunflower
ten feet tall!

The sun warms ponds
where fish eggs hatch.

And gives me lots
of fish to catch.

The sun warms turtles.
It warms frogs.

We love to lie
on sunny logs.

Bats and owls
stay out of it.

We don't like the sun
one bit.

It's good for lying in hammocks....

And splashing under hoses....

But don't stay out in the sun too long...

OIL

Too much is bad for noses.

Fireworks fill the sky!

Why?

Because July the fourth
is **THE FOURTH OF JULY**

It is also known as

INDEPENDENCE DAY

And on this day, we all say . . .

HAPPY BIRTHDAY USA

SUMMER BRINGS SUN AND FUN

swimming

floating

diving

boating

A bite! Look!

tanning

fanning

No hook!

outdoor cook

50

ACTUAL
FACTS
ABOUT
THUNDER
AND
LIGHTNING

Electricity
in your home
lights your lights.
It runs
the vacuum
for your mother.

Electricity
in the clouds
shoots
giant sparks
from one cloud
to another.

That's lightning.

Sometimes it's
pretty frightening.

When lightning flashes
from cloud to cloud,
it makes a noise
that's VERY loud.

If you wonder . . .
That's thunder.

KA-BOOOM

Something
to remember:
Summer ends
in September.

53

The next three months of the year are FALL

OCTOBER NOVEMBER DECEMBER

HOW WILL YOU KNOW IT'S FALL?

This is the time
of the Harvest Moon...

The time when the
caterpillar
makes his cocoon.

The weather
turns a little cool.

Some of us
are back in school.

2
+2

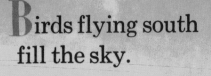

Birds flying south
fill the sky.

Summer plants
turn brown and dry.

There are lots
of pumpkins
and apples around.

There is a red and gold
carpet of leaves
on the ground.

So it must be
FALL!

October ends with **Halloween**...
Time for trick-or-treat.
We go out in funny clothes
and get good things to eat.

When is **Thanksgiving?**
Here's how to remember.
It's the fourth Thursday
That comes in November.

NOVEMBER

THANKSGIVING

turkey

stuffing

gravy

yams

rolls

butter

jellies

jams

corn

honey

hot mince pie

fruits

nuts

pumpkin pie

Father

Mother

Sister

Brother

... All are thankful for each other.

ACTUAL FACTS ABOUT
THE MOON

FULL MOON

Sometimes the moon
is round and bright.
It lights the way
for us at night.

CRESCENT MOON

On other nights
the moon is slim.
There is light.
But the light is dim.

NO MOON

It gets very, very dark
when there is no moon in sight.

If you go out
on nights like these,
be sure to take a light.

The moon looks like
a smooth round ball.
But a close look will show you
the moon's not smooth at all.

Some day soon,
you may go
to the moon .
You'll wave good-by
to your father and mother . . . .

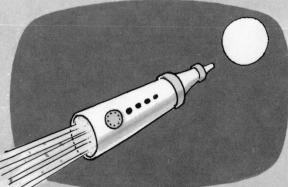

You'll rocket to the moon . . .

and get a moon rock
for your brother.

MOON ROCKS
5¢

In December,
friends,
Fall ends.

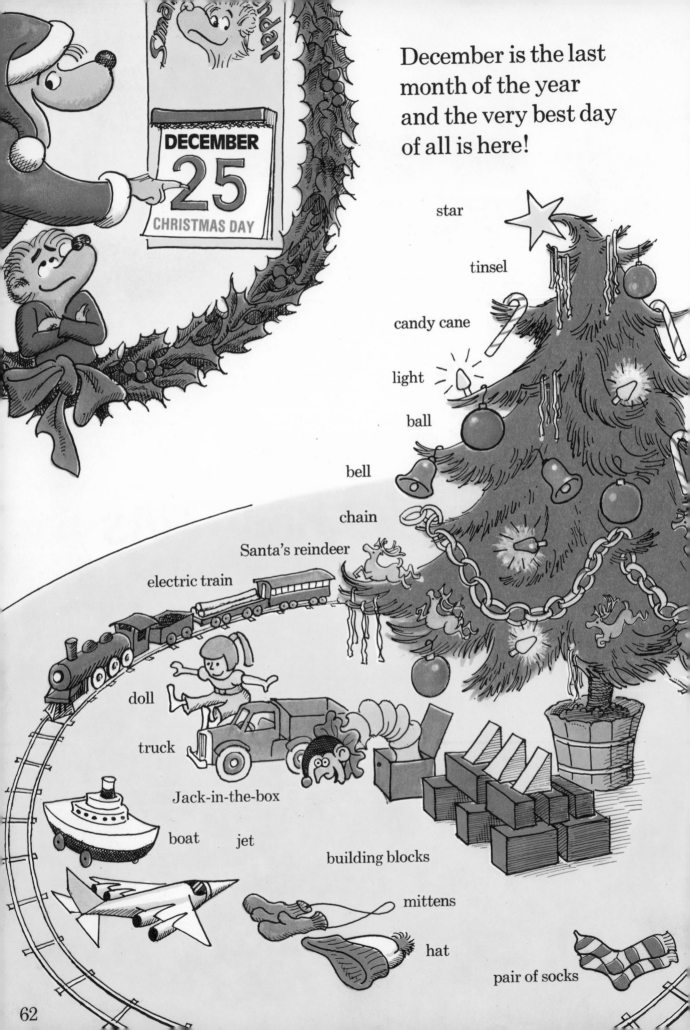

December is the last
month of the year
and the very best day
of all is here!

DECEMBER
25
CHRISTMAS DAY

star

tinsel

candy cane

light

ball

bell

chain

Santa's reindeer

electric train

doll

truck

Jack-in-the-box

boat   jet

building blocks

mittens

hat

pair of socks

62

cookies

fruit cake

candy bar

puzzle

book

wind-up car

stockings

sled

honey jar

On this day...

MERRY CHRISTMAS

is what we say!

ACTUAL FACTUAL BEAR

It's New Year's Eve!
A whole year ends.

Tomorrow we'll
start
a NEW YEAR
friends.

So, now, we can
all turn back
to the beginning
of our Almanac.

15 16 1446